REFLECTIONS
FOR
LENT 2024

REFLECTIONS
FOR
LENT

Wednesday 14 February –
Saturday 30 March 2024

ANDREW DAVISON
COLIN HEBER-PERCY
RACHEL MANN
MARK OAKLEY
RACHEL TREWEEK

with Holy Week reflections by
STEPHEN COTTRELL

Church House Publishing
Church House
Great Smith Street
London SW1P 3AZ

ISBN 978 1 78140 451 5

Published 2023 by Church House Publishing
Copyright © The Archbishops' Council 2023

The opinions expressed in this book are those of the
authors and do not necessarily reflect the official policy of
the General Synod or The Archbishops' Council of the
Church of England.

Liturgical editor: Peter Moger
Series editor: Hugh Hillyard-Parker
Designed and typeset by Hugh Hillyard-Parker
Copyedited by Ros Connelly
Printed and bound by CPI Group (UK) Ltd, Croydon, CR0 4YY

What do you think of *Reflections for Lent*?

We'd love to hear from you – simply email us at

publishing@churchofengland.org

or write to us at

Church House Publishing, Church House,
Great Smith Street, London SW1P 3AZ.

Visit **www.dailyprayer.org.uk** for more information
on the *Reflections* series, ordering and subscriptions.

Contents

About the authors   vi

About *Reflections for Lent*   1

Lent – jousting within the self   2
MARK OAKLEY

Building daily prayer into daily life   4
RACHEL TREWEEK

Lectio Divina – a way of reading the Bible   6
STEPHEN COTTRELL

Wednesday 14 February to Saturday 26 February   8
ANDREW DAVISON

Monday 28 February to Saturday 9 March   18
COLIN HEBER-PERCY

Monday 11 March to Saturday 23 March   30
RACHEL MANN

HOLY WEEK
Monday 25 March to Saturday 30 March   42
STEPHEN COTTRELL

Morning Prayer – a simple form   48

Seasonal Prayers of Thanksgiving   50

The Lord's Prayer and The Grace   51

An Order for Night Prayer (Compline)   52

About the authors

Stephen Cottrell is the Archbishop of York, having previously been Bishop of Chelmsford. He is a well-known writer and speaker on evangelism, spirituality and catechesis. He is one of the team that produced *Pilgrim*, the popular course for the Christian Journey.

Andrew Davison is the Starbridge Lecturer in Theology and Natural Sciences in the University of Cambridge, and Fellow in Theology and Dean of Chapel at Corpus Christi College. His publications include *Why Sacraments?*, *Participation in God*, *Astrobiology and Christian Doctrine*, and *The Love of Wisdom: An Introduction to Philosophy for Theologians*.

Colin Heber-Percy is an Anglican priest serving in the Salisbury Diocese. Before ordination, he was a screenwriter. His films and works for television won many awards and are shown all over the world. He writes and publishes regularly on theology and philosophy. His recent publications include *Perfect in Weakness*, on the cinema of Andrei Tarkovsky, and the bestselling *Tales of a Country Parish* which was published last year to critical acclaim.

Rachel Mann is an Anglican priest, writer and scholar. Author of eleven books, including her debut novel, *The Gospel of Eve*, and the Michael Ramsey Prize shortlisted, *Fierce Imaginings*, she is Visiting Fellow at the Manchester Writing School. She regularly contributes to *Pause For Thought* on BBC Radio Two, as well as other radio programmes. More info: www.rachelmann.co.uk

Mark Oakley is Dean and Fellow of St John's College, Cambridge, and Honorary Canon Theologian of Wakefield Cathedral in the Diocese of Leeds. He is the author of *The Collage of God* (2001), *The Splash of Words: Believing in Poetry* (2016), and *My Sour Sweet Days: George Herbert and the Journey of the Soul* (2019) as well as articles and reviews, in the areas of faith, poetry, human rights and literature. He is Visiting Lecturer in the department of Theology and Religious Studies at King's College London.

Rachel Treweek is Bishop of Gloucester and the first female diocesan bishop in England. She served in two parishes in London and was Archdeacon of Northolt and later Hackney. Prior to ordination she was a speech and language therapist and is a trained practitioner in conflict transformation.

About *Reflections for Lent*

Based on the *Common Worship Lectionary* readings for Morning Prayer, these daily reflections are designed to refresh and inspire times of personal prayer. The aim is to provide rich, contemporary and engaging insights into Scripture.

Each page lists the lectionary readings for the day, with the main psalms for that day highlighted in **bold**. The collect of the day – either the *Common Worship* collect or the shorter additional collect – is also included.

For those using this book in conjunction with a service of Morning Prayer, the following conventions apply: a psalm printed in parentheses is omitted if it has been used as the opening canticle at that office; a psalm marked with an asterisk may be shortened if desired.

A short reflection is provided on either the Old or New Testament reading. Popular writers, experienced ministers, biblical scholars and theologians contribute to this series, all bringing their own emphases, enthusiasms and approaches to biblical interpretation.

Regular users of Morning Prayer and *Time to Pray* (from *Common Worship: Daily Prayer*) and anyone who follows the Lectionary for their regular Bible reading will benefit from the rich variety of traditions represented in these stimulating and accessible pieces.

The book also includes both a simple form of Common Worship: Morning Prayer (see pages 48–49) and a short form of Night Prayer, also known as Compline (see pages 52–55), particularly for the benefit of those readers who are new to the habit of the Daily Office or for any reader while travelling.

Lent – jousting within the self

It has been said that the heart of the human problem is the problem of the human heart. Lent is time set aside each year to take this thought seriously.

A few years ago, there was a story in the papers about a painting by Pieter Bruegel the Elder. It is currently on display in Vienna's marvellous Kunsthistorisches Museum, but Krakow's National Museum claims it is theirs and that it was stolen by the wife of the city's Nazi governor in 1939 during the occupation of Poland.

The painting is called 'The Fight Between Carnival and Lent' and it was painted in 1559. It is a beautifully typical Bruegel painting. It is a large, crowded canvas with nearly 200 men, women and children depicted on it. We find ourselves looking down on a town square during a riotous festival. The painting can be looked at in two halves. On the right, we see a church with people leaving after prayer. We see them giving alms to the poor, feeding the hungry, helping those with disability, calling attention to their need and tending to the dying. On the left, we see an inn. Congregated around it are beer drinkers, gamblers, various saucy types. The vulnerable nearby are not noticed, including a solitary procession of lepers. Instead, a man vomits out of a window and another bangs his head against a wall.

In the foreground, we see two figures being pulled towards each other on floats. One is Lady Lent, gaunt and unshowy, dressed as a nun, with followers eating pretzels and fish as well as drawing fresh water from a large well. The other is Carnival, a fat figure, armed with a meat spit and a pork pie helmet. He's followed by masked carousers. A man in yellow – the symbolic colour of deceit – pushes his float, though he looks rather weighed down by cups and a bag of belongings. In the background, we see, on the left, some stark, leafless trees, but on the right side, buds are awakening on the branches and, as if to see them better, a woman is busily cleaning her windows.

It is an allegorical delight, and we might do worse than take a close look at it sometime this Lent. It's tempting to classify each human there as either good or bad, secular or faithful, kind or indifferent. We love to place people into convenient cutlery trays, dividing us all up as is most useful for us. What I love about this painting, however, is that it reminds me that we are all similarly made with two halves.

For so many of us, there is a constant fight going on within between the times we are negligent and the times we are careful; days in which we get through with a self that enjoys its own attention, being centre-stage, and days when our self just feels somehow more itself when not being selfish. I have an impulse to pray; I have an impulse to avoid or forget it. There are parts of me grotesquely masked, and there are parts of me trying to clean my windows on a ladder, as it were, wanting to increase transparency and attention to the world, to me and to my relationships.

Lent begins with a small dusty cross being made on my head, the hard case that protects the organ that makes decisions. The season starts by asking me to imagine how life might be if the imprint of Christ's courageous compassion might make itself felt and acted on, rather than just passionately talked about. Lent knows what we are like. It has seen the painting. It has read a bit of Freud, some history books, political manifestos and memoirs of hurt and achievement. It winces at our cyclical, self-destructive repetitions. It believes in us, though, knowing that, with God and each other, if we reach outside of our own hardened little worlds, we set the scene to be helped and, maybe, even changed. That would be good – for me and those who live with me.

In the Gospels, the 40 days Jesus spent in the beguiling wilderness immediately followed his baptism. Coming up out of the water, he had heard the unmistakable voice that matters, telling him he was cherished, wanted and ready. He then goes into the heat spending time with himself, hearing other voices that want him to live down to them; but he knows that his vocation can only be lived when he learns to live up to the one voice he heard that day in the river, not down to the ones that want him to live some conventionally indifferent and submerged existence as a consumer of the world and not as a citizen of the kingdom. We follow him. Where he goes, so do we. A wilderness Lent is needed more than ever to do some heart-repair and start becoming Christians again.

I don't know who owns the Bruegel painting. What I do know is that its themes belong to all of us; our inner landscape matches his rowdy town square. As long as the fight continues, the soul will be alive.

Mark Oakley

Building daily prayer into daily life

In our morning routines there are many tasks we do without giving much thought to them, and others that we do with careful attention. Daily prayer and Bible reading is a strange mixture of these. These are disciplines (and gifts) that we as Christians should have in our daily pattern, but they are not tasks to be ticked off. Rather they are a key component of our developing relationship with God. In them is *life* – for the fruits of this time are to be lived out by us – and to be most fruitful, the task requires both purpose and letting go.

In saying a daily office of prayer, we make a deliberate decision to spend time with God – the God who is always with us. In prayer and attentive reading of the Scriptures, there is both a conscious entering into God's presence and a 'letting go' of all we strive to control: both are our acknowledgement that it is God who is God.

> *… come before his presence with a song …*
>
> *Know that the Lord is God;*
> *it is he that has made us and we are his;*
> *we are his people and the sheep of his pasture.*
>
> *Enter his gates with thanksgiving …*
>
> *(Psalm 100, a traditional Canticle at Morning Prayer)*

If we want a relationship with someone to deepen and grow, we need to spend time with that person. It can be no surprise that the same is true between us and God.

In our daily routines, I suspect that most of us intentionally look in the mirror; occasionally we might see beyond the surface of our external reflection and catch a glimpse of who we truly are. For me, a regular pattern of daily prayer and Bible reading is like a hard look in a clean mirror: it gives a clear reflection of myself, my life and the world in which I live. But it is more than that, for in it I can also see the reflection of God who is most clearly revealed in Jesus Christ and present with us now in the Holy Spirit.

This commitment to daily prayer is about our relationship with the God who is love. St Paul, in his great passage about love, speaks of now seeing 'in a mirror, dimly' but one day seeing face to face: 'Now I know only in part; then I will know fully, even as I have been fully known' (1 Corinthians 13.12). Our daily prayer is part of that seeing in a mirror dimly, and it is also part of our deep yearning for an ever-clearer vision of our God. As we read Scripture, the past and the future converge in the present moment. We hear words from long ago – some of which can appear strange and confusing – and yet, the Holy Spirit is living and active in the present. In this place of relationship and revelation, we open ourselves to the possibility of being changed, of being reshaped in a way that is good for us and all creation.

It is important that the words of prayer and scripture should penetrate deep within rather than be a mere veneer. A quiet location is therefore a helpful starting point. For some, domestic circumstances or daily schedule make that difficult, but it is never impossible to become more fully present to God. The depths of our being can still be accessed no matter the world's clamour and activity. An awareness of this is all part of our journey from a false sense of control to a place of letting go, to a place where there is an opportunity for transformation.

Sometimes in our attention to Scripture there will be connection with places of joy or pain; we might be encouraged or provoked or both. As we look and see and encounter God more deeply, there will be thanksgiving and repentance; the cries of our heart will surface as we acknowledge our needs and desires for ourselves and the world. The liturgy of Morning Prayer gives this voice and space.

I find it helpful to begin Morning Prayer by lighting a candle. This marks my sense of purpose and my acknowledgement of Christ's presence with me. It is also a silent prayer for illumination as I prepare to be attentive to what I see in the mirror, both of myself and of God. Amid the revelation of Scripture and the cries of my heart, the constancy of the tiny flame bears witness to the hope and light of Christ in all that is and will be.

When the candle is extinguished, I try to be still as I watch the smoke disappear. For me, it is symbolic of my prayers merging with the day. I know that my prayer and the reading of Scripture are not the smoke and mirrors of delusion. Rather, they are about encounter and discovery as I seek to venture into the day to love and serve the Lord as a disciple of Jesus Christ.

+ Rachel Treweek

Lectio Divina – a way of reading the Bible

Lectio Divina is a contemplative way of reading the Bible. It dates back to the early centuries of the Christian Church and was established as a monastic practice by Benedict in the sixth century. It is a way of praying the Scriptures that leads us deeper into God's word. We slow down. We read a short passage more than once. We chew it over slowly and carefully. We savour it. Scripture begins to speak to us in a new way. It speaks to us personally, and aids that union we have with God through Christ, who is himself the Living Word.

Make sure you are sitting comfortably. Breathe slowly and deeply. Ask God to speak to you through the passage that you are about to read.

This way of praying starts with our silence. We often make the mistake of thinking prayer is about what we say to God. It is actually the other way round. God wants to speak to us. He will do this through the Scriptures. So don't worry about what to say. Don't worry if nothing jumps out at you at first. God is patient. He will wait for the opportunity to get in. He will give you a word and lead you to understand its meaning for you today.

First reading: Listen

As you read the passage listen for a word or phrase that attracts you. Allow it to arise from the passage as if it is God's word for you today. Sit in silence repeating the word or phrase in your head.

Then say the word or phrase aloud.

Second reading: Ponder

As you read the passage again, ask how this word or phrase speaks to your life and why it has connected with you. Ponder it carefully. Don't worry if you get distracted – it may be part of your response to offer to God. Sit in silence and then frame a single sentence that begins to say aloud what this word or phrase says to you.

Third reading: Pray

As you read the passage for the last time, ask what Christ is calling from you. What is it that you need to do or consider or relinquish or take on as a result of what God is saying to you in this word or phrase? In the silence that follows the reading, pray for the grace of the Spirit to plant this word in your heart.

If you are in a group, talk for a few minutes and pray with each other.

If you are on your own, speak your prayer to God either aloud or in the silence of your heart.

If there is time, you may even want to read the passage a fourth time, and then end with the same silence before God with which you began.

++Stephen Cottrell

Wednesday 14 February
Ash Wednesday

Psalm **38**
Daniel 9.3-6, 17-19
1 Timothy 6.6-19

1 Timothy 6.6-19
'... take hold of the life that really is life' (v.19)

The message of Lent is simple enough: 'take hold of the life that really is life.' The Greek for 'take hold' has a direct and earthy sense to it. It often means, literally, to grasp or seize something, and hold it tight. It can also mean 'take possession', in the sense of laying hold to a legal claim. Although there is nothing here to grasp with our hands, the message is to be as urgent about the faith, and the gospel, and the true life it offers, as if the seizing really were physical.

The imagery concerning hands is also there in the preceding verses, about the 'uncertainty of riches,' and the importance of being 'generous, and ready to share'. Recent neuroscience and psychology have underlined how much our thinking and language are based in our bodily experience and interaction with the world around us. One way to meditate on this passage – to 'get to grips with it', we might say – especially if there is no-one else around, might even be to enter into it with action or posture: miming or adopting a pose, such as opening and closing our hands, in some parts of holding firm (in relation to God and 'true life') and, in others, of letting go or sharing (in relation to what possessions we might enjoy). It is sometimes good to read the Bible with our whole body.

COLLECT

Almighty and everlasting God,
you hate nothing that you have made
and forgive the sins of all those who are penitent:
create and make in us new and contrite hearts
that we, worthily lamenting our sins
and acknowledging our wretchedness,
may receive from you, the God of all mercy,
perfect remission and forgiveness;
through Jesus Christ your Son our Lord,
who is alive and reigns with you,
in the unity of the Holy Spirit,
one God, now and for ever.

8 | *Reflection by* **Andrew Davison**

Psalm **77** *or* **37***
Genesis 39
Galatians 2.11-end

Thursday 15 February

Galatians 2.11-end

'... not by the works of the law but through faith in Jesus Christ'
(v.16)

Paul leaves us in no doubt that he is getting to the heart of the matter. He tells us that no one stands right with God or is put right with God (is 'justified') by doing the works of the law. Paul says that three times in a single verse, 'not by the works of the law but through faith in Jesus Christ... not by doing the works of the law, because no one will be justified by the works of the law' (v.16).

Historically, not least in the Protestant traditions, the great contrast here was thought to be between human actions and human faith: not 'works of the law', but 'faith in Jesus Christ'. Recent scholarship has highlighted an additional depth, so that what the NRSV translates here as 'faith *in* Jesus Christ' could be rendered 'the faith *of* Jesus Christ'. In that case, the contrast would not so much be between two things which belong to us – our faith *versus* our works of the law – but between anything at all that might originate with us, and what belongs to Christ, or between anything that we might do, and what Christ has done for us.

Especially if the 'faith in Jesus Christ' interpretation is the more familiar understanding for you, perhaps dwell today on the other: remembering that the message of grace is that Christ stands for us, and is faithful even when we are not.

Holy God,
our lives are laid open before you:
rescue us from the chaos of sin
and through the death of your Son
bring us healing and make us whole
in Jesus Christ our Lord.

COLLECT

Reflection by **Andrew Davison**

9

Friday 16 February

Galatians 3.1-14

*'Having started with the Spirit, are you now ending
with the flesh?' (v.3)*

Completion stands at the heart of the Passion story and the doctrine
of redemption. 'It is finished!' says Christ upon the cross, or
'completed!' – 'accomplished!' A variant of that word features in
one of Paul's outbursts of astonishment and grief in today's reading:
'Are you so foolish? Having started with the Spirit, are you now
ending with the flesh?' Or, as we might also translate it, 'Although
the Spirit started things off, are you now confident that the flesh will
bring things to completion?'

Paul is not down on the flesh. Christ redeemed us in and by his body.
Paul also writes that 'the life I now live in the flesh' (Galatians 2.20).
It is just that Paul no longer measures his life according to his own
actions or human accomplishments ('the flesh'), but by 'faith in the
Son of God [or faith in the faithfulness of Christ], who loved me and
gave himself for me'.

In this part of Galatians, 'flesh' is a problem because it stands for
confidence in our own actions. For the Galatians, that was notably
confidence in one particularly human action, namely circumcision.
As we make our way through Lent, Paul's challenge is for us to ask
how we try to justify ourselves to God, rather than accepting and
receiving God's justification of us by Christ.

C
O
L
L
E
C
T

Almighty and everlasting God,
you hate nothing that you have made
and forgive the sins of all those who are penitent:
create and make in us new and contrite hearts
that we, worthily lamenting our sins
and acknowledging our wretchedness,
may receive from you, the God of all mercy,
perfect remission and forgiveness;
through Jesus Christ your Son our Lord,
who is alive and reigns with you,
in the unity of the Holy Spirit,
one God, now and for ever.

Reflection by **Andrew Davison**

Psalm **71** *or* 41, **42**, 43
Genesis 41.1-24
Galatians 3.15-22

Saturday 17 February

Galatians 3.15-22

'Now a mediator involves more than one party; but God is one'
(v.20)

This is one most enigmatic sayings in all of Paul's letters. Writing in 1865, Bishop Lightfoot estimated '250 to 300' interpretations of it, not thinking much of most of them. Paul might be out to elevate the gospel over the law, since the law came through mediators, but the gospel from God directly, in Christ. Alternatively, the idea may be that mediations need to be negotiated and depend on the behaviour of both parties, while the grace of God in Christ has a glorious unilateral character to it: the gospel is so much more about God's faithfulness than it is about ours.

Alternatively, another commentator (Hans Dieter Betz, 1989) suggests that Paul's idea is that 'redemption requires conformity to the oneness of God.' On that, we can conclude with a magnificent passage from Augustine:

> Distracted and clinging to many things, it was necessary… that those same many things should join in proclaiming the One that should come… that, freed from the burden of many things, we should come to that One, and should love that One who, without sin, died in the flesh for us… that we should be justified by being made one in the one righteous One… and through Him as mediator, reconciled to God, cling to the One, feast upon the One, and remain one.

Holy God,
our lives are laid open before you:
rescue us from the chaos of sin
and through the death of your Son
bring us healing and make us whole
in Jesus Christ our Lord.

COLLECT

Monday 19 February

Psalms 10, 11 *or* 44
Genesis 41.25-45
Galatians 3.23 – 4.7

Galatians 3.23 – 4.7

'... all of you are one in Christ Jesus' (v.28)

In a justly celebrated line, Paul writes that 'There is no longer Jew or Greek, there is no longer slave or free, there is no longer male and female; for all of you are one in Christ Jesus.' The foundation for this is set out immediately before, namely membership of a new family, in which these diverse people 'all [become] children of God'. This new birth or adoption – here Paul speaks in terms of the latter – sets the running for all who belong to this family, trumping the accidents of natural birth.

The idea is also important in John's Gospel: 'to all who received him, who believed in his name, he gave power to become children of God, who were born, not of blood or of the will of the flesh or of the will of man, but of God' (John 1.13). As we might put it, the waters of baptism turn out to be thicker than blood.

The Church has taken its time in learning this lesson. That is an understatement. Even the great Augustine, commenting on our passage in one of his less impressive moments, wrote that although 'the unity of faith' teaches us 'that there are no such distinctions', nonetheless, 'within the orders of this life they persist', and in such matters it is best 'to avoid offence to others'. Surely, we are called to something more subversive than that!

COLLECT | Almighty God,
whose Son Jesus Christ fasted forty days in the wilderness,
and was tempted as we are, yet without sin:
give us grace to discipline ourselves in obedience to your Spirit;
and, as you know our weakness,
so may we know your power to save;
through Jesus Christ your Son our Lord,
who is alive and reigns with you,
in the unity of the Holy Spirit,
one God, now and for ever.

| *Reflection by* **Andrew Davison**

Psalm **44** *or* **48**, 52
Genesis 41.46 – 42.5
Galatians 4.8-20

Tuesday 20 February

Galatians 4.8-20

'... enslaved to beings that by nature are not gods' (v.4)

Taken by itself, this phrase could just about mean enslavement to fictional or imagined gods, precisely by following fictions. However, this is not the first time that Paul has mentioned supernatural beings in Galatians. Yesterday, we read 'we were enslaved to the elemental spirits of the world.' Paul surely therefore sees these beings as real, but counterfeit in comparison with the one God: they are more like angels, or the spirits of places, and seem of an evil character.

Pentecostal theology takes this sort of reference seriously. Elsewhere in Christianity, denial of angels and demons is not so prevalent as was a generation ago, but much academic theology still passes over these passages as something of an embarrassment, or at least strictly subordinate to a theology of justification, faith, grace, law, and so on. The tide might be turning. For a taste of Paul with these matters stressed and urgent, David Bentley Hart's recent translation of the New Testament is worth reading.

Looking on the wastes of twentieth-century history, Karl Barth insisted that we are bound to come under one power or another, and that this makes being under Christ good news. It belongs to 'divine mercy' that Christ should bring us under his 'lordship', because in that he 'delivers us from all other lordships' – including those 'beings' in Galatians – excluding once and for all their capacity to threaten us.

> Heavenly Father,
> your Son battled with the powers of darkness,
> and grew closer to you in the desert:
> help us to use these days to grow in wisdom and prayer
> that we may witness to your saving love
> in Jesus Christ our Lord.

COLLECT

Reflection by **Andrew Davison**   13

Wednesday 21 February

Galatians 4.21 – 5.1

'Hagar is Mount Sinai in Arabia and corresponds to the present Jerusalem' (v.25)

Here is Paul reflecting on a familiar story from the Book of Genesis. For anyone who likes their biblical interpretation sober, scholarly, and solidly grounded in the text, this passage is an eye-opener, even something of a scandal. Anyone who thinks the goal is to get back to something like the intention of the author, or what the first readers would have made of it, is not going to like this way to read Genesis.

Paul's method is allegory, where various parts of a story are taken to stand for (Paul says 'corresponds' to) something else. Allegory would become an important way to read the Bible, especially after the influence of the theological tradition coming out of Alexandria in Egypt in the early days of the Church, where allegory was as much in evidence among Jewish writers as Christian ones. Allegory would be influential for centuries to come, and here is Paul up to it too. How do we know when to take it seriously? After all, we could use an allegory to make almost any text mean anything.

A rule sprang up that we should not read any passage of the Bible in this 'non-literal' way when it can be justified by the literal reading of some other passage. Christians are forever drawing on the Bible to make creative allusions. (If you are using Common Worship Daily Prayer, look at the canticle refrains.) You may do it yourselves. When is that legitimate, and when are we playing fast and loose? It's responsible whatever what we're saying is in accord with how the point is covered, more straightforwardly, elsewhere in the Bible: which is how Paul uses allegory here.

COLLECT

Almighty God,
whose Son Jesus Christ fasted forty days in the wilderness,
and was tempted as we are, yet without sin:
give us grace to discipline ourselves in obedience to your Spirit;
and, as you know our weakness,
so may we know your power to save;
through Jesus Christ your Son our Lord,
who is alive and reigns with you,
in the unity of the Holy Spirit,
one God, now and for ever.

Reflection by **Andrew Davison**

Psalms **42**, 43 *or* 56, **57** (63*)
Genesis 42.18-28
Galatians 5.2-15

Thursday 22 February

Galatians 5.2-15

'... the only thing that counts is faith working through love' (v.6)

We have read a good deal so far in Galatians about various words or categories that history has strongly associated with Paul, and rightly so: faith and works, grace and law. With today's reading, a fifth word bursts onto the scene, one that we should recognise as being as equally central to Paul's lexicon as any of the others, namely *love*.

One of the seemingly great disagreements in the New Testament is between Paul, elevating faith over works, and James, writing that works are what makes faith real. With talk of 'faith working through love', however, as Bishop Lightfoot put it, those words 'bridge over the gulf which seems to separate the language of St Paul and St James. Both assert a principle of practical energy, as opposed to a barren, inactive theory.'

The problem is perhaps that we treat faith in a more cognitive and individual way than what it intended in either the Old Testament or the New. Consider Abraham, the great paradigm of faith. His faith was, above all, trust in God. Unlike self-justifying works, it was all about God. And yet that trust wasn't purely internal, or about assenting to ideas. It is seen in leaving his home, and in raising the knife to sacrifice his son. Precisely because faith is most of all trust, it is inseparable from love.

Heavenly Father,
your Son battled with the powers of darkness,
and grew closer to you in the desert:
help us to use these days to grow in wisdom and prayer
that we may witness to your saving love
in Jesus Christ our Lord.

COLLECT

Reflection by **Andrew Davison** | 15

Friday 23 February

Psalm **22** *or* **51**, 54
Genesis 42.29-end
Galatians 5.16-end

Galatians 5.16-end

'There is no law against such things' (v.23)

Paul's Letter to the Galatians has its grumpy moments, but if the mood is often tense, that is because of Paul's love for the Galatians, and his fears about what they stand to lose. The tone is often fraught, but then along comes one of the sunniest passages in the whole of the Bible: the list of the fruit of the Spirit.

Just as, yesterday, love emerged as the final answer to the relation of grace and works, so these fruits lift us out of theological wrangles about the role and status of the law, since 'there is no law against such things.' Paul's contrast is between flesh and spirit. It's important to recognise that this is not a judgement on the body as such, or some denigration of materiality. 'Flesh' and 'Spirit' are two ways of living in its entirety. There is a led-by-the-Spirit way of being a bodily creature, and a 'fleshly' way of being abstractly spiritual and disdainful of creation.

Although the word 'grace' does not feature in the reading today, it lies at the heart what is going on here. By grace, God truly gives us what he gives – such as these fruits – and, in that, they do not spring from our own efforts or deserving, but from God's gracious gift.

COLLECT

Almighty God,
whose Son Jesus Christ fasted forty days in the wilderness,
and was tempted as we are, yet without sin:
give us grace to discipline ourselves in obedience to your Spirit;
and, as you know our weakness,
so may we know your power to save;
through Jesus Christ your Son our Lord,
who is alive and reigns with you,
in the unity of the Holy Spirit,
one God, now and for ever.

Reflection by **Andrew Davison**

Saturday 24 February

Galatians 6

'Bear one another's burdens' (v.2)

If we were looking for a contradiction in the New Testament, we seem to find one here: 'Bear one another's burdens' (v.2), but 'all must carry their own loads' (v.5). Something interesting must be going on. Here are three suggestions from various commentaries.

First, the 'burdens' in v.2 seem to be associated with sin and temptation (v.1). If so, then we do well to be pastorally generous with others, but strict with ourselves. 'Do not judge', Christ says, but, he adds, be aware that you will be judged by God.

Second, the words in the two verses are different. Usage varies, but burden' in v.2 puts the emphasis on heaviness and weight. In contrast, while the 'load' in v.5 is certainly not easy, it seems to be the sort of burden that we all have to carry in daily life. As elsewhere, therefore, Paul is keen to stress that Christian charity is no excuse for shirking one's everyday responsibilities (2 Thessalonians 3.10).

Finally, we might notice that in v.5 Paul seems to be simply repeating some well-worn Greek maxim, praising the sort of self-sufficiency familiar to any Stoic philosopher. On the other hand, v.2 looks of Paul's own making. As elsewhere, Paul does not disparage Greek wisdom, but the newness of love offers the yet 'more excellent way' (1 Corinthians 12.31) than anything known before.

COLLECT

Heavenly Father,
your Son battled with the powers of darkness,
and grew closer to you in the desert:
help us to use these days to grow in wisdom and prayer
that we may witness to your saving love
in Jesus Christ our Lord.

Reflection by **Andrew Davison**   17

Monday 26 February

Psalms 26, **32** *or* **71**
Genesis 43.16-end
Hebrews 1

Hebrews 1

'Long ago...' (v.1)

No 'Paul, a servant of Jesus Christ... to all God's beloved' or 'Paul, called to be an apostle of Christ... to the Church of God'. No introduction, no greeting, no indication that this is an epistle at all. Instead we are plunged straight into a theological treatise on the cosmic Christ.

Who wrote the Epistle to the Hebrews? God alone knows. So says Origen, writing in the mid third century. Origen suspects it might have been written by Clement, the third Bishop of Rome (c.35–100). And to whom is this letter addressed? 'To the Hebrews' is a later Christian best guess, based on the way the text draws so extensively on Old Testament sources and seeks to reveal Christ as their fulfilment.

And this lacing together of past and present, of 'long ago' to 'these last days', is our key to the text, and to our understanding of Hebrews' Christology. Christ is a 'reflection', a turning back, a perfect mirroring of God's glory; he is an exact 'imprint', a fixing of God's very being in the now; and he 'sustains all things' into the future. His throne 'is for ever and ever', embracing all time.

The 'Epistle to the Hebrews' sets out to remind us: the Bible is a book, bound, with a spine. It tells one story, beginning, middle and end: Christ. This is not for Hebrews then or Gentiles now. It is for all. For ever.

COLLECT

Almighty God,
you show to those who are in error the light of your truth,
that they may return to the way of righteousness:
grant to all those who are admitted
    into the fellowship of Christ's religion,
that they may reject those things
    that are contrary to their profession,
and follow all such things as are agreeable to the same;
through our Lord Jesus Christ,
who is alive and reigns with you,
in the unity of the Holy Spirit,
one God, now and for ever.

Reflection by **Colin Heber-Percy**

Psalm **50** *or* **73**
Genesis 44.1-17
Hebrews 2.1-9

Tuesday 27 February

Hebrews 2.1-9

'Pay greater attention' (v.1)

Attention costs. We have to pay for it. Or do we? Like so much else in our world, attention has become a transaction. Our attention is valuable, measured these days in clicks, likes and shares.

But the word in the Greek of Hebrews that is translated here as 'pay attention to' is actually better rendered as 'hold to' or 'attend to' or even 'devote oneself to'. We are called to hold fast that which we have heard, lest we 'drift away'. This message is a life preserver. Not something for which we pay, but something which has been thrown to us, and for us. It is salvation.

In Matthew's Gospel, when Peter steps out of the boat he notices the wind and waves. Frightened, he starts to sink (Matthew 14.28-33). Think of the storms and travails in our own lives. We feel we are sinking. Perhaps we feel ourselves drifting away. Peter cries out, and Jesus takes him by the hand.

We are unable to win the salvation to which we are called, or pay for it or merit it, but we can see it in the saving action of Jesus Christ, walking towards us.

To be saved is first to be spent; to be found we must have been lost. Recognising that we are adrift and unable to save ourselves is the first step. 'Lord, save me!' (Matthew 14.30).

And hold fast.

Almighty God,
by the prayer and discipline of Lent
may we enter into the mystery of Christ's sufferings,
and by following in his Way
come to share in his glory;
through Jesus Christ our Lord.

COLLECT

Reflection by **Colin Heber-Percy**   19

Wednesday 28 February

Hebrews 2.10-end

'... to become like his brothers and sisters' (v.17)

Six and a half thousand hymns written in one lifetime is an extraordinary feat. But this is the final tally of human hymnal, Charles Wesley (1707–88). While most of his hymns are now forgotten, many are still cherished. Think of 'Love divine...' or 'And can it be...' But arguably the best loved of all is 'Hark! The herald angels sing'.

Perhaps it was Monday's reading from Hebrews, with its reference to angels as 'spirits in divine service' (Hebrews 1.14) that has put me in mind of Wesley's carol. The line, 'veiled in flesh, the Godhead see' is taken by many to be unorthodox. They say it implies a divine Christ hidden behind the human Jesus, that Jesus of Nazareth is God's disguise. But what if the revelation *is* the veil, is made possible *by* the veil? After all, a screen separates, but it also displays. And a cinema without a screen, without a veil, would be useless. Jesus is not God's disguise, but God's self-disclosure.

Wesley's line suggests we can see the godhead only when it is veiled, *because* it is veiled. Likewise, for the writer of Hebrews, incarnation is identification. The deity becomes like us 'in every respect'. Flesh and the thousand natural shocks it is heir to, becomes the means whereby we are saved through God's atoning action in Christ Jesus.

We are saved, not from sufferings, but '*through* [his] sufferings'. He suffered – in the flesh – for us.

COLLECT

Almighty God,
you show to those who are in error the light of your truth,
that they may return to the way of righteousness:
grant to all those who are admitted
    into the fellowship of Christ's religion,
that they may reject those things
    that are contrary to their profession,
and follow all such things as are agreeable to the same;
through our Lord Jesus Christ,
who is alive and reigns with you,
in the unity of the Holy Spirit,
one God, now and for ever.

Reflection by **Colin Heber-Percy**

Psalm **34** *or* **78.1-39***
Genesis 45.1-15
Hebrews 3.1-6

Thursday 29 February

Hebrews 3.1-6

'... we are his house' (v.6)

Tucked into the courtyard of San Pietro in Montorio on the Gianicolo in Rome is the Tempietto, the Little Temple. Designed by Bramante in the early sixteenth century, the Tempietto is supposed to be built over the site of St Peter's crucifixion. It is tiny, more sculpture than building, a dummy run for Bramante's big commission – St Peter's basilica. Despite its being so small, and so hard to find, the Tempietto is a masterpiece of Renaissance Italian architecture.

The most significant feature of the building is also the most immediately obvious: it is perfectly circular, which means no aspect of this temple is more important than any other. Nothing is obscured behind an imposing façade. There is no backstage. No cheap seats. No grand apartments, no servants' quarters. No forgotten corners.

In his letter to the Ephesians, Paul talks of us being 'built together spiritually into a dwelling-place for God' (Ephesians 2.22). We are called to be built into a living, unified whole. This is not a temple we enter; we *are* the temple, his house. And as such, we are a circle, like the Tempietto, with Christ as the keystone, holding us together as 'holy partners in a heavenly calling'.

Walls divide. And in a wall, the stones or bricks are often all the same. In this circle, there are no dividing walls; and each stone – each 'partner', each Peter – is cut and dressed to serve a unique loving purpose.

Almighty God,
by the prayer and discipline of Lent
may we enter into the mystery of Christ's sufferings,
and by following in his Way
come to share in his glory;
through Jesus Christ our Lord.

COLLECT

Friday 1 March

Hebrews 3.7-end

'... as long as it is called "today"' (v.13)

You are reading these words today. How could it be otherwise? And yet I am writing these words to be read on a day that will be 'today' only for a brief twenty-four hours sometime in my future. Our passage for this twenty-four hours is concerned with history and time. We are urged to 'hold our first confidence firm to the end'. From yesterday, through today, and into tomorrow.

But this holding must not become a hardening. Hardening is related to sinfulness and rebellion and unbelief. Instead, we are called to 'hear his voice' and to remain obedient. Elsewhere, Paul commands us to 'stand firm and hold to the traditions which you were taught' (2 Thessalonians 2.15). And our word 'tradition' means – at its Latin root – to hand over, to hand on, or to surrender.

To hold today to the faith tradition of our ancestors does not mean we are backward looking. Precisely the opposite. We do not look back *to* the past, we look out *from* the past. For God 'has put a sense of past and future into [our] minds, yet [we] cannot find out what God has done from the beginning to the end' (Ecclesiastes 3.11). To try to find out, to put God to the test is to break the terms of our surrender, and to harden.

In faith, and as partners of Christ we live today. And it is always today.

COLLECT

Almighty God,
you show to those who are in error the light of your truth,
that they may return to the way of righteousness:
grant to all those who are admitted
    into the fellowship of Christ's religion,
that they may reject those things
    that are contrary to their profession,
and follow all such things as are agreeable to the same;
through our Lord Jesus Christ,
who is alive and reigns with you,
in the unity of the Holy Spirit,
one God, now and for ever.

| *Reflection by* **Colin Heber-Percy**

Psalms 3, **25** *or* **76**, 79
Genesis 46.1-7, 28-end
Hebrews 4.1-13

Saturday 2 March

Hebrews 4.1-13

'... his rest is still open' (v.1)

'Busy' is often our stock answer to the question, 'How are you?' or 'How are things?' We take pride in our being busy. It suggests we are wanted, in demand, and unavailable. A busy phone line means our call cannot be answered. 'All our operators are busy right now...'

To be busy is to be restless. And, as Augustine prays in the opening chapter of his *Confessions*, 'our hearts are restless till they rest in you.' In our restlessness and distraction, we are operators, conformed to the business of the world.

Our ancestors, as the writer of Hebrews makes clear, were not listening, were disobedient, and therefore failed to find rest. In short, they had closed themselves to the good news that comes to us and offers rest.

We think of rest as taken or earned. But here rest is *entered*. Paradoxically, to enter this rest takes effort. There are six days before the Sabbath, but those six days find their point and their end in rest. Likewise, our efforts and our toil make sense only with rest as their reward.

The call in this passage is to make every effort to remain faithful and obedient to the promised rest that is the meaning of our lives, our sole purpose and end.

If busy is closed, rest remains open. Ultimately, we are never restless. Our call will be taken, and heard.

Almighty God,
by the prayer and discipline of Lent
may we enter into the mystery of Christ's sufferings,
and by following in his Way
come to share in his glory;
through Jesus Christ our Lord.

COLLECT

Reflection by **Colin Heber-Percy** | 23

Monday 4 March

Psalms **5**, 7 *or* **80**, 82
Genesis 47.1-27
Hebrews 4.14 – 5.10

Hebrews 4.14 – 5.10
'... a great high priest' (4.14)

In my early twenties I attended a church where the vicar would use this passage as an invitation to confession: 'Seeing we have a great high priest who has passed into the heavens...' After one service, I approached the vicar and asked, 'Who is this great high priest?' I imagined some eminent prelate had recently gone to their reward. The vicar looked at me. 'Jesus,' he said. 'Jesus is our great high priest.' What? I had never imagined Jesus as a high priest. And truth be told, I still don't, or not often.

We tend to think of Jesus as a baby in a manger, or as an inspired and itinerant teacher, as a charismatic leader, innocent victim of oppression or/and as the Messiah, Christ, Son of God. But a priest? Surely, as representatives of religious and temporal authority, the priests are those whom Jesus comes to confront with their hypocrisy and worldly values? How can we think of him as 'one of them'?

But priesthood, as defined in this passage, is sacrificial and vocational; it demands obedience and 'reverent submission'. So Jesus is not just a priest, but the very model and measure of a universal and cosmic priesthood. That we are unable to attain to the perfection of this model is the point. We don't have to. He has 'in every respect been tested, as we are' so that *through him* we may 'receive mercy and find grace'.

COLLECT

Almighty God,
whose most dear Son went not up to joy
    but first he suffered pain,
and entered not into glory before he was crucified:
mercifully grant that we, walking in the way of the cross,
may find it none other than the way of life and peace;
through Jesus Christ your Son our Lord,
who is alive and reigns with you,
in the unity of the Holy Spirit,
one God, now and for ever.

Reflection by **Colin Heber-Percy**

Tuesday 5 March

Hebrews 5.11 – 6.12

'... unskilled in the word of righteousness' (5.13)

Is righteousness a skill we can learn, a faculty we can train? We are used to thinking of Christianity as having less to do with our understanding, however dull it may be, and more to do with faith and love. There is a danger in this: that we make our faith fluffy in an effort to render it palatable for all, more widely appealing and 'relevant'.

Writing in the seventeenth century, Brother Lawrence says in *The Practice of the Presence of God* that 'We must know before we can love.' Knowledge or understanding is a prerequisite.

A new member of a Bible study group confessed to me recently that she felt uncomfortable after an evening meeting. 'You're all so much further on in your faith than I am,' she said. I found myself trying to allay her fears by suggesting there is no 'further on' in faith, that we are all learning all the time. While this may not be false, there was, I now suspect, a hint of disingenuousness in my answer.

Because, according to Hebrews, we *can* progress – by diligence, practice, and imitation – from infancy to maturity, from milk to solid food. And we do this through attention to the teaching, through learning, through knowing stuff.

By ducking difficult questions and skirting complexities we may be in danger of watering down 'the word of righteousness' and our theological tradition, offering milk when the world is hungry for solid food.

Eternal God,
give us insight
to discern your will for us,
to give up what harms us,
and to seek the perfection we are promised
in Jesus Christ our Lord.

COLLECT

Wednesday 6 March

Hebrews 6.13-end

'... behind the curtain' (v.19)

When Dorothy pulls aside the curtain in Oz's throne room she finds, not a mighty wizard, but an ordinary bloke with a microphone. Faith in the wizard turns out to be 'smoke and mirrors'; it is groundless.

When we swear an oath, we swear on that which is greater than ourselves. That which is greater than us acts as surety, as guarantor, as ground. But, as St Anselm puts it, 'God is that than which nothing greater can be conceived.' So who underwrites God's promise? God, according to our passage. Is this not like Baron Munchausen pulling himself out of the swamp by his own hair? Or me pulling myself up by my bootstraps? If I draw the curtain aside, will I find something Oz-ish, unsupported and arbitrary? Smoke and mirrors?

While 'all things are possible with God' (Matthew 19.26; Mark 10.27), there remains a class of actions not open to God (or any other agent). These are not actions which, as a matter of fact, God cannot perform; they are things logically impossible, like constructing a circle that has corners.

God is not true to his word; God *is* the truth. So 'it is impossible that God would prove false'. For God's promise to prove false would be for God not to be God. This is not a proof, but a promise. A promise *as person* preceding us and entering 'the shrine behind the curtain'.

COLLECT

Almighty God,
whose most dear Son went not up to joy
    but first he suffered pain,
and entered not into glory before he was crucified:
mercifully grant that we, walking in the way of the cross,
may find it none other than the way of life and peace;
through Jesus Christ your Son our Lord,
who is alive and reigns with you,
in the unity of the Holy Spirit,
one God, now and for ever.

Reflection by **Colin Heber-Percy**

Psalms **56**, 57 *or* 90, **92**   **Thursday 7 March**
Genesis 49.33 – end of 50
Hebrews 7.1-10

Hebrews 7.1-10

'... without genealogy' (v.3)

Surely Melchizedek is a walk on, a supporting artist, an extra? Apart from this fleeting, two verse passage from Genesis (14.18-20) to which the writer of Hebrews refers, only one other mention of Melchizedek occurs in the Old Testament. In Psalm 110 we find, 'You are a priest forever according to the order of Melchizedek.' And that's it. So what does the writer find in these brief glimpses of an obscure King of Salem that is so vital?

Psalm 110 is the most cited psalm in the New Testament (mainly here in Hebrews). Glorying in the victory of God's priest-king, the psalm was taken by Christians from the earliest days to tell of Christ's coming in judgement and power.

Whereas Matthew and Luke in their Gospels are keen to provide a genealogy for Jesus, establishing him as a scion of the house of David, the writer of Hebrews places that which is superior outside of history. Melchizedek's authority rests in his being 'without father, without mother, without genealogy'. Melchizedek comes to occupy a transcendent position, beyond time and space, in virtue of his having no history. No 'begats' precede him or follow him; he is lineage-less.

This shadowy extra in the narrative of scripture turns out to be the threshold between God and the world, between transcendence and immanence, between promise and fulfilment. And Christ is the one who steps across that threshold.

Eternal God,
give us insight
to discern your will for us,
to give up what harms us,
and to seek the perfection we are promised
in Jesus Christ our Lord.

COLLECT

Reflection by **Colin Heber-Percy**   27

Friday 8 March

Psalm **22** *or* **88** (95)
Exodus 1.1-14
Hebrews 7.11-end

Hebrews 7.11-end

'... approach God' (v.19)

How do we approach God? Through the law, or through the Life? Presenting the argument of Hebrews as a dichotomy like this does a deep disservice to the text, and raises the spectre of antisemitism that has had disastrous consequences throughout European history. In short, Hebrews does not rehearse an argument against Judaism, but within Judaism.

A superficial and specious reading of Hebrews might suggest the author points to a turning over of the Temple, an abandoning of the old dispensation, and an abrogation of the law. Rather than advocating severance or schism, however, the writer talks of change. 'When there is a change in the priesthood, there is necessarily a change in the law.' This is not inevitably a total break with tradition or the law, but a new way of belonging to that tradition and abiding by that law.

In fact, Hebrews out-conserves the conservatives by attesting to the validation of Christ Jesus' priestly ministry according to the order of Melchizedek. The Epistle to the Hebrews offers, not something radically new, but something radically old, and better: a 'better hope', a 'better covenant'.

How do we approach God? Through a better hope, a saving promise. And this will demand our relying, not on priests to offer gifts and make sacrifices on our behalf 'day after day' but by relying today and always on him, the high priest who offered himself as sacrifice once for all.

COLLECT

Almighty God,
whose most dear Son went not up to joy
   but first he suffered pain,
and entered not into glory before he was crucified:
mercifully grant that we, walking in the way of the cross,
may find it none other than the way of life and peace;
through Jesus Christ your Son our Lord,
who is alive and reigns with you,
in the unity of the Holy Spirit,
one God, now and for ever.

Reflection by **Colin Heber-Percy**

Psalm **31** *or* 96, **97**, 100
Exodus 1.22 – 2.10
Hebrews 8

Saturday 9 March

Hebrews 8

'... a sketch and shadow' (v.5)

A few years ago, at an exhibition of Raphael's drawings, I was captivated by a sketch of the resurrection. People's bodies, tumbling away from the tomb like victims in an explosion, express shock, wonder, and fear. The deft sketch was made on a discarded piece of paper into which a compass point had previously been pressed. Turning over the page, Raphael used the compass's puncture hole as the inspiration and focus of his new composition. The empty hole in the page, like the empty tomb, becomes like a singularity at the heart-start of a Big Bang. 'I am about to do a new thing; now it springs forth, do you not perceive it?' (Isaiah 43.19).

What was obsolete disappears by being turned over, like a page, what was damaged becomes the entry point for the faultless. It would be hard to find a better illustration of the meaning of the resurrection, or the message of Hebrews with its call for us to recognise the transcendence of Christ, our high priest who has 'now obtained a more excellent ministry.'

The 'sketch and shadow' of this world with its laws and temples and traditions is suddenly and explosively pierced with 'a new covenant', a new truth. There is no longer need for teaching or for the law to command 'Know the Lord' for we have been turned over, and what was damage is now blessing, what was an end is now a beginning.

Eternal God,
give us insight
to discern your will for us,
to give up what harms us,
and to seek the perfection we are promised
in Jesus Christ our Lord.

COLLECT

Monday 11 March

Hebrews 9.1-14

'Christ came as a high priest of the good things...' (v.11a)

The Letter to the Hebrews is charged with powerful imagery. Jesus is both great high priest and Son of God. This theologically exciting vision of Christ can be intimidating. Then a phrase which draws one deeper into mystery: 'Christ came as a high priest of the good things that have come'. For all the highly ritualised and cosmic language which speaks of Jesus entering once for all into the holy place to obtain eternal redemption with his blood, we can rest in the knowledge that he is the priest of the good things. What might they be? Surely these are the things which flow out of restored relationship and intimacy with God: forgiveness and friendship; refreshed love and hope, and the breaking down of all that might separate us from the love of God.

Indeed, the offer of intimacy with God himself, in and through Jesus, is the greatest thing. Through Christ we are invited to re-enter and renew our place as people of gift: we are invited to recognise that all we have comes from God and the only appropriate response is thanksgiving and praise. For in Christ, we are not separated from the good things of God, but discover that such good things are our abiding dwelling place. For all the high falutin language, Christ's love calls us home. We discover that our home is found in our dwelling-place with God.

Merciful Lord,
absolve your people from their offences,
that through your bountiful goodness
we may all be delivered from the chains of those sins
which by our frailty we have committed;
grant this, heavenly Father,
for Jesus Christ's sake, our blessed Lord and Saviour,
who is alive and reigns with you,
in the unity of the Holy Spirit,
one God, now and for ever.

| *Reflection by* **Rachel Mann**

Exodus 2.23 – 3.20
Hebrews 9.15-end

Tuesday 12 March

Hebrews 9.15-end

'He is the mediator of a new covenant...' (v.15a)

Many scholars have suggested that Hebrews was written to a group of persecuted Jewish Christians tempted to give up following Jesus. If that view has been questioned in recent scholarship, one cannot avoid how Jesus is seemingly presented as the one who supersedes the Jewish gift of law and covenant. He is 'the mediator of a new covenant'. When Hebrews was likely to have been composed, the dynamics between Jewish and Gentile Christians were complex. Nonetheless, two thousand years on, in the light of millennia of anti-semitism, stoked and often facilitated by bad readings of the Christian scriptures, there are fresh challenges when we speak of a new covenant.

This is not the place to attempt a deep dive into Hebrews' place in anti-semitic discourse. It is possible, however, to claim a rich understanding of Jesus as the mediator of a new covenant without trashing the old. We read that Jesus 'has appeared once for all at the end of the age to remove sin by the sacrifice of himself'. Christ's self-sacrifice is an invitation for us to encounter God's redemptive love poured out for all. Nonetheless, I have long believed that, in Christ, non-Jews are grafted into an older Jewish story of God's love and salvation. Old and new Covenant are not in competition, but reveal the abiding desire of God for all to be in deep reconciled relationship with him and one another.

Merciful Lord,
you know our struggle to serve you:
when sin spoils our lives
and overshadows our hearts,
come to our aid
and turn us back to you again;
through Jesus Christ our Lord.

COLLECT

Reflection by **Rachel Mann** | 31

Wednesday 13 March

Psalms 63, **90** or 110, **111**, 112
Exodus 4.1-23
Hebrews 10.1-18

Hebrews 10.1-18

'... every priest stands day after day at his service' (v.11)

Hebrews is rich with the language of priesthood. While its writer is at pains to emphasise the cosmic power of Christ's priesthood at the expense of Old Testament priesthood, the Letter is, nonetheless, an invitation to reflect deeply on the meaning of priestly vocation.

For many of us, whether ordained or not, reflecting on priesthood and vocation too readily resolves into what it means to be a 'dog-collar wearer' or not. However, it is worth reminding ourselves that we are all – through baptism – part of what St Peter calls the priesthood of all believers. This royal priesthood, formed in Jesus Christ, is shaped by service and love. Those who follow Jesus are not called to lord it over others, but to be liberated into service as our Lord serves: 'by a single offering he has perfected for all time those who are sanctified.' This is not the 'holier than thou' perfection of the self-satisfied, but the humility of those who have been liberated to become their true selves.

As one of the 'dog-collar' variety of priests, I am only too conscious that being a priest is one of the ways Christ has called me into loving service. It is Christ who really matters, though. Ultimately, priesthood is the way God holds me and calls me into life. The royal priesthood of all believers flows from Jesus Christ, the priest of all creation.

COLLECT

Merciful Lord,
absolve your people from their offences,
that through your bountiful goodness
we may all be delivered from the chains of those sins
which by our frailty we have committed;
grant this, heavenly Father,
for Jesus Christ's sake, our blessed Lord and Saviour,
who is alive and reigns with you,
in the unity of the Holy Spirit,
one God, now and for ever.

| *Reflection by* **Rachel Mann**

Psalms 53, **86** *or* 113, **115**
Exodus 4.27 – 6.1
Hebrews 10.19-25

Thursday 14 March

Hebrews 10.19-25

'... let us consider how to provoke one another to love and good deeds' (v.24)

Provocation is not a word one hears very often in church. More often than not we talk of relationship, peace, love, and forgiveness. Provocation appears aggressive; being provocative is something many Christians avoid.

There is something arresting, then, about how the Letter to the Hebrews dares to suggest that there is a place for it. The Letter's first audience is exhorted not only to persevere in its devotion without wavering and to come into God's fellowship with a 'true heart in full assurance of faith', but to find a place for provocation.

'And let us consider how to provoke one another to love and good deeds...' Provocation here might also mean to stimulate or stir-up. However, I like the intensity of the word provocation. It has implications of 'incite' and 'call forth'. I suspect many of us hear such words in connection with acts of violence, or calling forth anger or division. In Hebrews the people of God are invited to incite and call one another to love and good deeds.

We live in challenging times, in both the Church and the wider world. We are exhausted and the world is weary too. We, like the Letter's original audience, might be tempted to neglect 'to meet together' and connect as we ought. Perhaps it's time we were all a bit more provocative. Certainly, the world could do with more love and good deeds.

COLLECT

Merciful Lord,
you know our struggle to serve you:
when sin spoils our lives
and overshadows our hearts,
come to our aid
and turn us back to you again;
through Jesus Christ our Lord.

Reflection by **Rachel Mann**   33

Friday 15 March

Hebrews 10.26-end

'It is a fearful thing to fall into the hands of the living God' (v.31)

'Where will you spend eternity? Heaven or hell?' When I was a curate I walked past those lines, printed on a poster in an underpass, every day on my way to church. Though memorable, the questions did not encourage me in my faith. I think the Christian Fellowship that had posted it thought it would motivate readers to follow Jesus. It was a 'gotcha'. While I too want people to come to faith in Jesus, to me the poster read as a cheap threat.

Threats can motivate, but typically only by generating fear of consequences. Today's passage certainly holds its share of threat. It suggests that those in the Christian community who spurn Jesus will deserve a punishment so harsh it will make the death meted out to those who spurned Moses pale into insignificance.

Fear, of course, has multiple meanings. Today's passage says, 'it is a fearful thing to fall into the hands of the living God.' For me, the fearful reality of God generates awe rather than anxiety. The living God is genuinely awesome. If threat is implied, the threat of the living God applies to our craven schemes and desires. The living God 'threatens' us with the fullness of life and love; he offers an opportunity to walk into the fullness of life. Will we have the courage to take that path?

COLLECT

Merciful Lord,
absolve your people from their offences,
that through your bountiful goodness
we may all be delivered from the chains of those sins
which by our frailty we have committed;
grant this, heavenly Father,
for Jesus Christ's sake, our blessed Lord and Saviour,
who is alive and reigns with you,
in the unity of the Holy Spirit,
one God, now and for ever.

| *Reflection by* **Rachel Mann**

Psalms **32** *or* 120, **121**, 122
Exodus 7.8-end
Hebrews 11.1-16

Saturday 16 March

Hebrews 11.1-16

'Faith is the assurance of things hoped for, the conviction of things not seen' (v.1)

In recent years there has been a huge upsurge of interest in tracing one's family tree. The 'ancestry industry' has become vast; searching for family history has never been easier. Perhaps, in these uncertain times and the ongoing societal retreat from organised religion, searching for one's family tree can offer a form of reassurance. A family tree can make one feel as if one has a history and a story to which one / we belong(s).

Scripture, too, has more than its fair share of genealogies, including the genealogy of Jesus in Matthew's Gospel. The Bible doesn't shy away from ancestors and today's reading invites us to meditate on the witness of our forebears in faith.

However, Abraham, Sarah *et al.* are not presented as causes of hope simply because they are ancestors. They matter because of what they reveal about faith. They show that faith involves living by promises and walking into hope. This is a costly way, for, as our forebears in faith reveal, we shall not, in this life, all reach the promised land. Still, we are invited to persist, for faith is 'the assurance of things hoped for'.

Faith is, I think, like planting a tree: one may not live to see it grow to full maturity, but still we plant it, in promise and hope. Faith requires trust: trust that, no matter what, God will bring the tree of goodness to its full flowering.

> Merciful Lord,
> you know our struggle to serve you:
> when sin spoils our lives
> and overshadows our hearts,
> come to our aid
> and turn us back to you again;
> through Jesus Christ our Lord.

COLLECT

Reflection by **Rachel Mann**   35

Monday 18 March

Psalms **73**, 121 *or* 123, 124, 125, **126**
Exodus 8.1-19
Hebrews 11.17-31

Hebrews 11.17-31

'...he persevered as though he saw him who is invisible' (v.27b)

Over the past decade, I've had the privilege of working on various projects with theatre creatives. One of the things I've learned is how much the 'end product' – the performance – depends on the preparation. Rehearsal time is crucial; through repetition and reflection, a theatre company not only tests what can be wrung out from the script, but what that script looks like when it is 'put it on its feet', as they say, in real time. Rehearsal can be inspiring, tedious, tense, and hilarious. Theatre creatives want to offer a great end-product, but that simply won't happen without rehearsal.

Today's reading presents a form of rehearsal. The story of God's people is repeated over and over; as the motif 'by faith' is repeated, the hearer is invited deeper into the story. We are invited into the unfolding history of faith, discerning fresh nuance in its rehearsal.

The writer's use of a repeated motif is an example of the classic rhetorical device, *anaphora*. It's a technique used by poets, playwrights and, indeed, politicians, to aid memorability and underline what matters. While such a technique can be used – especially in the hands of a skilled public speaker – to whip up a crowd or bypass independent thought, when it is used to rehearse the story of God's pilgrim people we draw closer to God. We find our place more fully in God's definitive story.

COLLECT

Most merciful God,
who by the death and resurrection of your Son Jesus Christ
delivered and saved the world:
grant that by faith in him who suffered on the cross
we may triumph in the power of his victory;
through Jesus Christ your Son our Lord,
who is alive and reigns with you,
in the unity of the Holy Spirit,
one God, now and for ever.

Reflection by **Rachel Mann**

Psalms 25, 147.1-12
Isaiah 11.1-10
Matthew 13.54-end

Tuesday 19 March
Joseph of Nazareth

Matthew 13.54-end

'Is not this the carpenter's son?' (v.55a)

Joseph of Nazareth is a beautifully ambiguous saint. As Jesus' adoptive father, he is clearly a key figure in Christ's story, yet he is also a marginal one. His role is overshadowed, not least, by that of the Blessed Virgin Mary. Joseph operates both in the margins and in the main text of the Jesus story.

When the villagers ask, 'Is not this the carpenter's son?', I hear something of both shock and put-down. They imply not only that Jesus' true identity is bound up with and limited by his earthly father's, but also that Jesus' authority is no more than that of a carpenter's son.

However, Joseph's adoptive parenthood reconfigures familial authority and relationship in fresh and hopeful ways. He *is* Jesus' father; however, this is parenthood which holds space for Jesus to inhabit his full divine identity, not restricted by traditional social convention.

As we grow into the likeness of Christ, we too are invited to dwell ever more fully in the household of God. While many of us do have rich and nourishing experiences of family, it is by no means so for all. Perhaps part of what makes God's richer conception of family so potent is that there is always space at its heart for those of us, like Joseph, who seemingly have walk-on parts in the kingdom of heaven.

COLLECT

God our Father,
who from the family of your servant David
raised up Joseph the carpenter
to be the guardian of your incarnate Son
and husband of the Blessed Virgin Mary:
give us grace to follow him
in faithful obedience to your commands;
through Jesus Christ your Son our Lord,
who is alive and reigns with you,
in the unity of the Holy Spirit,
one God, now and for ever.

Reflection by **Rachel Mann**

Wednesday 20 March

Psalms **55**, 124 *or* **119.153-end**
Exodus 9.1-12
Hebrews 12.3-13

Hebrews 12.3-13

'Endure trials for the sake of discipline' (v.7)

I am just about old enough to remember the use of corporal punishment in schools. One image in particular is seared in my memory: the trembling distress and shame of an eleven-year-old boy in my class after he was slippered in front of us by the teacher. When I read of God disciplining or punishing his people like children, I instinctively balk at the idea. I associate discipline with violence and injustice. I go back to that scene in the classroom.

Perhaps a healthier way of seeing discipline is in terms of the call to discipleship. To grow as a disciple requires a willingness to adapt and shift. I've only met one person on my Christian journey who is the finished article and that's Jesus. When Hebrews says, 'God is treating you as children; for what child is there whom a parent does not discipline?', that question does not necessarily contain a suggestion of violence. The fact is that no child can hope to find her way in this world if she is totally feral; parents know that a child needs guidance.

I'm unconvinced that God deliberately sends trials to test and form us. However, in the company of that most loving parent, God, we have a faithful companion. In the midst of life's inevitable trials, he is present; not to diminish or hurt, but to show us the way to grow through them into the likeness of Christ.

COLLECT | Most merciful God,
who by the death and resurrection of your Son Jesus Christ
delivered and saved the world:
grant that by faith in him who suffered on the cross
we may triumph in the power of his victory;
through Jesus Christ your Son our Lord,
who is alive and reigns with you,
in the unity of the Holy Spirit,
one God, now and for ever.

| *Reflection by* **Rachel Mann**

Psalms **40**, 125 *or* **143**, 146
Exodus 9.13-end
Hebrews 12.14-end

Thursday 21 March

Hebrews 12.14-end

'See to it that no one fails to obtain the grace of God...' (v.15)

When I was a callow curate, my training incumbent said something which has stayed with me, 'The Church attracts the best and the worst.' I think I said in response, 'And sometimes the best and worst is contained in the same person.' My colleague's simple statement reminds us that we shouldn't be surprised if disagreements and bitter division break out in church: it reflects human life in all its pettiness, poverty, and, sometimes, its promise. Community includes saints and sinners.

The Letter to the Hebrews warns its readers to guard against the growth of bitterness among the community of God. That warning surely applies as much to the Church today. Given the messiness of human nature, and our capacity for division, it's difficult, especially if one feels hard done by, for some to resist the temptation to bitterness. I've certainly been tempted when I've felt the Church has been unjust in its treatment of LGBT+ people like me.

Nonetheless, as people of faith we are invited to live out an extraordinary challenge: 'See to it that no one fails to obtain the grace of God.' It is a command to leave no one behind. In particular, for those of us who exercise leadership in the Church, it is a command which should give us pause, for there is no appropriate collateral damage and no acceptable wastage in the kingdom of God.

COLLECT

Gracious Father,
you gave up your Son
out of love for the world:
lead us to ponder the mysteries of his passion,
that we may know eternal peace
through the shedding of our Saviour's blood,
Jesus Christ our Lord.

Reflection by **Rachel Mann** | 39

Friday 22 March

Psalms **22**, 126 *or* 142, **144**
Exodus 10
Hebrews 13.1-16

Hebrews 13.1-16

'Do not neglect to show hospitality to strangers...' (v.2)

'Do not neglect to show hospitality to strangers, for by doing that some have entertained angels without knowing it.' Rightly, this is one of the Bible's most famous lines. It invites its readers to be rich in hospitality. Here, in the depths of the New Testament, is a call-back to that extraordinary encounter between Abraham and the three visitors at Mamre in Genesis 18. In that encounter Abraham and Sarah meet, in the three strangers, the very presence of God. When we are gracious to strangers, we can meet the living God.

This all sounds wonderful in principle. The Greek word used for stranger in this passage can mean foreigner or alien. However, it is increasingly clear that in many nations today there is, either consciously or unconsciously, often a distinction between good and bad foreigners. Some, such as those who have fled Ukraine, are seen as good; others as bad. Politicians and nations may or may not have sound criteria for discerning between those who are welcome to enter its community. However, the Bible is much more challenging. It asks people of faith to centre their lives on grace. Crucially, we are called to commit to forms of hospitality focussed on those outside or on the edge of the community. When we follow that path, we might entertain angels unawares.

COLLECT

Most merciful God,
who by the death and resurrection of your Son Jesus Christ
delivered and saved the world:
grant that by faith in him who suffered on the cross
we may triumph in the power of his victory;
through Jesus Christ your Son our Lord,
who is alive and reigns with you,
in the unity of the Holy Spirit,
one God, now and for ever.

Reflection by **Rachel Mann**

Psalms **23**, 127 *or* **147**
Exodus 11
Hebrews 13.17-end

Saturday 23 March

Hebrews 13.17-end

'May the God of peace… make you complete in everything good'
(vv.20-21a)

In the light of Church abuse scandals – scandals centred on how those who hold power exploit the vulnerable – I blanch when I read 'Obey your leaders and submit to them, for they are keeping watch over your souls and will give an account.' Certainly, Hebrews was written in a context different to our own, with its own disciplinary challenges, but still we must read it in the context of our own Church.

Ultimately, however, it is the conclusion of Hebrews which brings us back to heart of the matter: we are called to be centred on the living God who is the God of peace. The crucial closing words of the letter constitute a benediction which invites God – the one who brought back from the dead our Lord Jesus, the great shepherd of the sheep – to make us complete in everything good.

Benediction means nothing more or less than 'speaking good'. I wish we, in the Church today, were more committed to blessing and speaking good of one another. Not because we are naïve about our power problems or are determined to let off a proper accountability those who've done wicked things, but because ultimately, we shall find our final, definitive identity in Jesus Christ. Ultimately, we shall stand before him. In this life, a little more benediction may help us do his will, that we may work among us all that is pleasing in his sight.

Gracious Father,
you gave up your Son
out of love for the world:
lead us to ponder the mysteries of his passion,
that we may know eternal peace
through the shedding of our Saviour's blood,
Jesus Christ our Lord.

COLLECT

Monday 25 March
Monday of Holy Week

Psalm 41
Lamentations 1.1-12*a*
Luke 22.1-23

Lamentations 1.1-12*a*

'O Lord, look at my affliction, for the enemy has triumphed!' (v.9)

As we walk towards the cross this week, we are summoned to stand there and see the depth and cost of God's love for us in Christ.

Probably written by the prophet Jeremiah who witnessed the fall of Jerusalem in 586 BC, the poems of sorrow, despair and devastation which make up the book of Lamentations have an always been used by the Church to help tell the story of Christ's death. Verses from Lamentations are sung on Good Friday; and particularly this verse, 'Is it nothing to you, all you who pass by? Look and see if there is any sorrow like my sorrow' (v.12), invites us to get inside the story of Christ's passion and the sorrow he carries.

Just as Jerusalem is described as being like a widow weeping, so the Church stands at the cross and weeps for the death of Christ. And even though we know this is not the end of the story, we have to get inside the reality of Christ's death and the meaning of his passion in order to fully receive and understand the resurrection. Therefore, we need to be brought to a place of weeping. And often it is the poems, the music and the drama of our liturgy that helps us to do this.

Jeremiah himself is sometimes called the weeping prophet. This week we are called to be weeping disciples.

COLLECT

Almighty and everlasting God,
who in your tender love towards the human race
    sent your Son our Saviour Jesus Christ
to take upon him our flesh
and to suffer death upon the cross:
grant that we may follow the example of his patience and humility,
and also be made partakers of his resurrection;
through Jesus Christ your Son our Lord,
who is alive and reigns with you,
in the unity of the Holy Spirit,
one God, now and for ever.

   Reflection by **Stephen Cottrell**

Psalm 27
Lamentations 3.1-18
Luke 22. [24-38] 39-53

Tuesday 26 March
Tuesday of Holy Week

Lamentations 3.1-18

'I have become the laughing-stock of all my people' (v.14)

Sometimes we read these Old Testament passages and it seems as if they describe the passion of Jesus. Other examples would be Psalm 22 or Isaiah 53. In this case it is almost as if Jesus is speaking to us himself from the cross: 'my flesh and my skin waste away...' (v.4); 'I have become a laughing stock...' (v.14); 'my soul is bereft of peace...' (v.17). But what is particularly disturbing here is that it is *God* who has brought about these travails. '*He* has filled me with bitterness' (v.15) says the writer of Lamentations.

In the context of the fall of Jerusalem, it is clear that this desolation and exile has been brought upon God's people because of their disobedience and faithlessness. But we can't say this of Jesus, the one who is obedient to God in all things.

No, Jesus *chooses* the way of faithful obedience, even to suffering and death. He plumbs the depths of what it is to be human. He carries our sorrows and failings. He even experiences abandonment from God as he cries out in Mark's Gospel, 'Why have you forsaken me?' (Mark 15.34). He experiences the terrible consequences of sin and death, but is without sin himself. He does this for us.

True and humble king,
hailed by the crowd as Messiah:
grant us the faith to know you and love you,
that we may be found beside you
on the way of the cross,
which is the path of glory.

COLLECT

Reflection by **Stephen Cottrell**   43

Wednesday 27 March
Wednesday of Holy Week

Psalm 102 [*or* 102.1-18]
Wisdom 1.16 – 2.1; 2.12-22
or Jeremiah 11.18-20
Luke 22.54-end

Jeremiah 11.18-20

'I was like a gentle lamb led to the slaughter' (v.19)

The first Christians came to believe that Jesus suffered, died and rose again *in accordance with* the scriptures – a phrase that pops up in scripture itself and in the Nicene Creed which many of us say each week. So when Paul tells the story of his conversion, he insists that he is 'saying nothing but what the prophets and Moses said would come to pass: that the Christ must suffer and… rise from the dead' (Acts 26.22,23). Therefore, they looked at the Old Testament passages that spoke of a suffering servant, or in today's case, 'a gentle lamb led to the slaughter' (v.19), and saw in them a foreshadowing of what God had done for us in Jesus. They then tell the story with reference to these passages.

John's Gospel, for instance, begins with John the Baptist saying, 'Look, there is the Lamb of God' (John 1.29). You could argue that the whole Gospel is then told to help us discover what that means; that what happened to Jesus was according to God's purposes from the beginning, and that Jesus is the Passover Lamb who takes our sins away.

Jesus does commit his cause to the Lord (v.20). He is vindicated. But it is *through* suffering and death, not around it. In these next few days we find out what that means.

T C E L L O C	Almighty and everlasting God, who in your tender love towards the human race sent your Son our Saviour Jesus Christ to take upon him our flesh and to suffer death upon the cross: grant that we may follow the example of his patience and humility, and also be made partakers of his resurrection; through Jesus Christ your Son our Lord, who is alive and reigns with you, in the unity of the Holy Spirit, one God, now and for ever.

Reflection by **Stephen Cottrell**

Psalms 42, 43
Leviticus 16.2-24
Luke 23.1-25

Thursday 28 March
Maundy Thursday

Leviticus 16.2-24

'Thus he shall make atonement...' (v.16)

The book of Leviticus gives careful and precise instructions for how the priests are to conduct the sacrifices in the Temple that, in the sacrifice of Jesus, are rendered superfluous. But they also help us to understand that sacrifice. In this case Jesus himself is become the 'scapegoat' upon whom other people's sins and transgressions are piled.

How does this work? How can Jesus carry my sins? How can he forgive what other people have done wrong? After all, he isn't the victim?

The answer lies on the cross. And since it is true that only the one who has been wronged has the right to forgive, Jesus, the one person who is without sin, becomes, as it were, the ultimate victim. He carries my sinfulness. And its consequence.

On the night before he dies, breaking bread and sharing wine, Jesus shows his friends how his death will be a sacrifice, an offering of himself, his body broken, his blood shed. It is a kind of 'acted parable'. The disciples didn't understand it at the time. How could they? But days later they remembered – and carried on remembering.

For those of us who follow Jesus, this astonishing good news of God's forgiveness is renewed and its benefits given to us in the sacrifice of the Eucharist. We, too, remember. And as this evening falls, Christian people across the world will gather and make this Eucharist, this remembrance, together.

True and humble king,
hailed by the crowd as Messiah:
grant us the faith to know you and love you,
that we may be found beside you
on the way of the cross,
which is the path of glory.

COLLECT

Reflection by **Stephen Cottrell**   45

Friday 29 March
Good Friday

Psalm 69
Genesis 22.1-18
Hebrews 10.1-10

Genesis 22.1-18

'On the mount of the Lord it shall be provided' (v.14)

These anxious and uncomprehending words of Isaac to his father Abraham, echo down the centuries, 'The fire and the wood are here, but where is the lamb for a burnt-offering?' And they find their fulfilment in Jesus.

Abraham is being asked to do something unimaginably horrific, to sacrifice his own son. Trusting, but also uncomprehending, Abraham replies, 'God himself will provide the lamb for a burnt-offering, my son' (v.8). He cannot imagine that this will be fulfilled upon the cross. At the terrible moment as he draws the knife, he sees a ram caught in as thicket and presumes this is what God meant. But the real understanding is found in St John's account of the passion of Jesus, the account that is read in most churches across the world at the Good Friday liturgy today. Departing from Matthew, Mark and Luke's chronology where Jesus is crucified on the day after the Passover, in John's Gospel Jesus is crucified on the day of the festival itself; and John times the crucifixion precisely so that it takes place at the same time as the Passover lambs are being sacrificed in the Temple. The point is plain. Jesus is the true Passover lamb. The Lord has provided. And carrying his own cross, Jesus is obedient to death. By his wounds, we are healed.

COLLECT

Almighty Father,
look with mercy on this your family
for which our Lord Jesus Christ was content to be betrayed
    and given up into the hands of sinners
    and to suffer death upon the cross;
who is alive and glorified with you and the Holy Spirit,
one God, now and for ever.

Reflection by **Stephen Cottrell**

Psalm 142
Hosea 6.1-6
John 2.18-22

Saturday 30 March
Easter Eve

Hosea 6.1-6

'Let us press on to know the Lord; his appearing is as sure as the dawn' (v.3)

Holy Saturday. The day after. And the day before. The bleakest, loneliest day of the year. The emptiest day. All our hopes buried.

Jesus is dead. And Jesus is not yet risen.

It's hard for us to get inside this day. We are busy polishing brass and arranging lilies for tomorrow's celebrations. But today is the one day of the year when there is no water in the font. We are called to wait for the Lord.

And even if we can't imaginatively lay aside our knowledge of the resurrection, and even if we are busy, it is good to wait. Even for a few moments. For even if we believe that Christ is risen there will be other doubts and sorrows inside us. And provided we don't keep pressing them down, they will find voice in today's scriptures. For our love for God is often like morning mist that quickly disappears. And we are forever making deals with God – or at least trying to! – when what God wants from us is steadfast love.

He has done away with sacrifices now. And he will come to us like the spring showers that water the earth, he will heal us and bind us up.

All this is waiting for us. And we must wait too.

Come, let us return to the Lord.

Grant, Lord,
that we who are baptized into the death
of your Son our Saviour Jesus Christ
may continually put to death our evil desires
and be buried with him;
and that through the grave and gate of death
we may pass to our joyful resurrection;
through his merits,
who died and was buried and rose again for us,
your Son Jesus Christ our Lord.

COLLECT

Morning Prayer – a simple form

Preparation

O Lord, open our lips
and our mouth shall proclaim your praise.

A prayer of thanksgiving for Lent *(for Passiontide see p. 50)*

Blessed are you, Lord God of our salvation,
to you be glory and praise for ever.
In the darkness of our sin you have shone in our hearts
to give the light of the knowledge of the glory of God
in the face of Jesus Christ.
Open our eyes to acknowledge your presence,
that freed from the misery of sin and shame
we may grow into your likeness from glory to glory.
Blessed be God, Father, Son and Holy Spirit.
Blessed be God for ever.

Word of God

Psalmody *(the psalm or psalms listed for the day)*

Glory to the Father and to the Son
and to the Holy Spirit;
as it was in the beginning is now:
and shall be for ever. Amen.

Reading from Holy Scripture *(one or both of the passages set for the day)*

Reflection

The Benedictus (The Song of Zechariah) *(see opposite page)*

Prayers

Intercessions – a time of prayer for the day and its tasks, the world and its need, the church and her life.

The Collect for the Day

The Lord's Prayer *(see p. 51)*

Conclusion

A blessing or the Grace *(see p. 51)*, or a concluding response

Let us bless the Lord
Thanks be to God

Benedictus *(The Song of Zechariah)*

1   Blessed be the Lord the God of Israel, ♦
    who has come to his people and set them free.

2   He has raised up for us a mighty Saviour, ♦
    born of the house of his servant David.

3   Through his holy prophets God promised of old ♦
    to save us from our enemies,
        from the hands of all that hate us,

4   To show mercy to our ancestors, ♦
    and to remember his holy covenant.

5   This was the oath God swore to our father Abraham: ♦
    to set us free from the hands of our enemies,

6   Free to worship him without fear, ♦
    holy and righteous in his sight
        all the days of our life.

7   And you, child, shall be called the prophet of the Most High, ♦
    for you will go before the Lord to prepare his way,

8   To give his people knowledge of salvation ♦
    by the forgiveness of all their sins.

9   In the tender compassion of our God ♦
    the dawn from on high shall break upon us,

10 To shine on those who dwell in darkness
        and the shadow of death, ♦
    and to guide our feet into the way of peace.

Luke 1.68-79

**Glory to the Father and to the Son
and to the Holy Spirit;
as it was in the beginning is now:
and shall be for ever. Amen.**

Seasonal Prayers of Thanksgiving

Passiontide

Blessed are you, Lord God of our salvation,
to you be praise and glory for ever.
As a man of sorrows and acquainted with grief
your only Son was lifted up
that he might draw the whole world to himself.
May we walk this day in the way of the cross
and always be ready to share its weight,
declaring your love for all the world.
Blessed be God, Father, Son and Holy Spirit.
Blessed be God for ever.

At Any Time

Blessed are you, creator of all,
to you be praise and glory for ever.
As your dawn renews the face of the earth
bringing light and life to all creation,
may we rejoice in this day you have made;
as we wake refreshed from the depths of sleep,
open our eyes to behold your presence
and strengthen our hands to do your will,
that the world may rejoice and give you praise.
Blessed be God, Father, Son and Holy Spirit.
Blessed be God for ever.

after Lancelot Andrewes (1626)

The Lord's Prayer and The Grace

Our Father in heaven,
hallowed be your name,
your kingdom come,
your will be done,
on earth as in heaven.
Give us today our daily bread.
Forgive us our sins
as we forgive those who sin against us.
Lead us not into temptation
but deliver us from evil.
For the kingdom, the power,
and the glory are yours
now and for ever.
Amen.

(or)

Our Father, who art in heaven,
hallowed be thy name;
thy kingdom come;
thy will be done;
on earth as it is in heaven.
Give us this day our daily bread.
And forgive us our trespasses,
as we forgive those who trespass against us.
And lead us not into temptation;
but deliver us from evil.
For thine is the kingdom,
the power and the glory,
for ever and ever.
Amen.

The grace of our Lord Jesus Christ,
and the love of God,
and the fellowship of the Holy Spirit,
be with us all evermore.
Amen.

An Order for Night Prayer (Compline)

Preparation

The Lord almighty grant us a quiet night and a perfect end.
Amen.

Our help is in the name of the Lord
who made heaven and earth.

A period of silence for reflection on the past day may follow.

The following or other suitable words of penitence may be used

**Most merciful God,
we confess to you,
before the whole company of heaven and one another,
that we have sinned in thought, word and deed
and in what we have failed to do.
Forgive us our sins,
heal us by your Spirit
and raise us to new life in Christ. Amen.**

O God, make speed to save us.
O Lord, make haste to help us.

**Glory to the Father and to the Son
and to the Holy Spirit;
as it was in the beginning is now
and shall be for ever. Amen.
Alleluia.**

The following or another suitable hymn may be sung

Before the ending of the day,
Creator of the world, we pray
That you, with steadfast love, would keep
Your watch around us while we sleep.

From evil dreams defend our sight,
From fears and terrors of the night;
Tread underfoot our deadly foe
That we no sinful thought may know.

O Father, that we ask be done
Through Jesus Christ, your only Son;
And Holy Spirit, by whose breath
Our souls are raised to life from death.

The Word of God

Psalmody

One or more of Psalms 4, 91 or 134 may be used.

Psalm 134

1   Come, bless the Lord, all you servants of the Lord, ♦
      you that by night stand in the house of the Lord.

2   Lift up your hands towards the sanctuary ♦
      and bless the Lord.

3   The Lord who made heaven and earth ♦
      give you blessing out of Zion.

Glory to the Father and to the Son
and to the Holy Spirit;
as it was in the beginning is now
and shall be for ever. Amen.

Scripture Reading

One of the following short lessons or another suitable
passage is read

You, O Lord, are in the midst of us and we are called by your
name; leave us not, O Lord our God.

Jeremiah 14.9

(or)

Be sober, be vigilant, because your adversary the devil is
prowling round like a roaring lion, seeking for someone
to devour. Resist him, strong in the faith.

1 Peter 5.8,9

(or)

The servants of the Lamb shall see the face of God, whose name
will be on their foreheads. There will be no more night: they will
not need the light of a lamp or the light of the sun, for God will
be their light, and they will reign for ever and ever.

Revelation 22.4,5

The following responsory may be said

Into your hands, O Lord, I commend my spirit.
Into your hands, O Lord, I commend my spirit.
For you have redeemed me, Lord God of truth.
I commend my spirit.
Glory to the Father and to the Son
and to the Holy Spirit.
Into your hands, O Lord, I commend my spirit.

Or, in Easter

Into your hands, O Lord, I commend my spirit.
Alleluia, alleluia.
Into your hands, O Lord, I commend my spirit.
Alleluia, alleluia.
For you have redeemed me, Lord God of truth.
Alleluia, alleluia.
Glory to the Father and to the Son
and to the Holy Spirit.
Into your hands, O Lord, I commend my spirit.
Alleluia, alleluia.

Keep me as the apple of your eye.
Hide me under the shadow of your wings.

Gospel Canticle

Nunc Dimittis (The Song of Simeon)

Save us, O Lord, while waking,
and guard us while sleeping,
that awake we may watch with Christ
and asleep may rest in peace.

1   Now, Lord, you let your servant go in peace:
    your word has been fulfilled.

2   My own eyes have seen the salvation
    which you have prepared in the sight of every people;

3   A light to reveal you to the nations
    and the glory of your people Israel.

Luke 2.29-32

54

**Glory to the Father and to the Son
and to the Holy Spirit;
as it was in the beginning is now
and shall be for ever. Amen.**

**Save us, O Lord, while waking,
and guard us while sleeping,
that awake we may watch with Christ
and asleep may rest in peace.**

Prayers

Intercessions and thanksgivings may be offered here.

The Collect

Visit this place, O Lord, we pray,
and drive far from it the snares of the enemy;
may your holy angels dwell with us and guard us in peace,
and may your blessing be always upon us;
through Jesus Christ our Lord.
Amen.

The Lord's Prayer (see p. 51) may be said.

The Conclusion

In peace we will lie down and sleep;
for you alone, Lord, make us dwell in safety.

Abide with us, Lord Jesus,
for the night is at hand and the day is now past.

As the night watch looks for the morning,
so do we look for you, O Christ.

[Come with the dawning of the day
and make yourself known in the breaking of the bread.]

The Lord bless us and watch over us;
the Lord make his face shine upon us and be gracious to us;
the Lord look kindly on us and give us peace.
Amen.

Love what you've read?

Why not consider using *Reflections for Daily Prayer* all year round? We also publish these meditations on Bible readings in an annual format, containing material for the entire Church year.

The volume for 2024/25 will be published in May 2024 and features contributions from a host of distinguished writers including: **Justine Allain Chapman, Kate Bruce, Tom Clammer, Maggi Dawn, Luigi Gioia, Malcolm Guite, Liz Hoare, Libby Lane, John Inge, Michael Ipgrave, Graham James, Jan McFarlane, Mark Oakley, John Perumbalath, John Pritchard, Sarah Rowland Jones, Brother Sam SSF, Rachel Treweek** and **Catherine Williams**.

The reflections for Holy Week 2025 are written by **Paula Gooder**.

**Reflections for Daily Prayer:
Advent 2024 to the eve of Advent 2025**

ISBN 978 1 78140 457 7
Available May 2024

Can't wait for next year?

You can still pick up this year's edition of *Reflections*, direct from us (at **www.chpublishing.co.uk**) or from your local Christian bookshop.

**Reflections for Daily Prayer:
Advent 2023 to the eve of Advent 2024**

ISBN 978 1 78140 395 2
£16.99 • Available now

REFLECTIONS FOR DAILY PRAYER
App

Make Bible study and reflection a part of your routine wherever you go with the Reflections for Daily Prayer App for Apple and Android devices.

Download the app for free from the App Store (Apple devices) or Google Play (Android devices) and receive a week's worth of reflections free. Then purchase a monthly, three-monthly or annual subscription to receive up-to-date content.

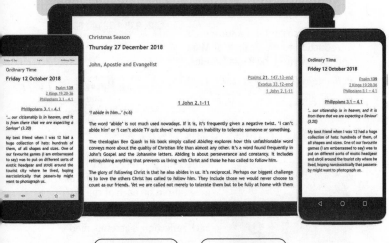

REFLECTIONS FOR SUNDAYS (YEAR B)

Reflections for Sundays offers over 250 reflections on the Principal Readings for every Sunday and major Holy Day in Year B, from the same experienced team of writers that have made *Reflections for Daily Prayer* so successful. For each Sunday and major Holy Day, they provide:

- full lectionary details for the Principal Service
- a reflection on each Old Testament reading (both Continuous and Related)
- a reflection on the Epistle
- a reflection on the Gospel.

This book also contains a substantial introduction to the Gospels of Mark and John, written by **Paula Gooder**.

Reflections for Sundays is also available in separate volumes for **Years A** and **C**.

£16.99 • 288 pages
ISBN 978 1 78140 030 2

Also available in Kindle and epub formats

REFLECTIONS ON THE PSALMS

£14.99 • 192 pages
ISBN 978 0 7151 4490 9

Reflections on the Psalms provides original and insightful meditations on each of the Bible's 150 Psalms.

Each reflection is accompanied by its corresponding Psalm refrain and prayer from the *Common Worship Psalter*, making this a valuable resource for personal or devotional use.

Specially written introductions by **Paula Gooder** and **Steven Croft** explore the Psalms and the Bible and the Psalms in the life of the Church.